REMARKABLE RESCUES

Books in the FACT ATTACK series

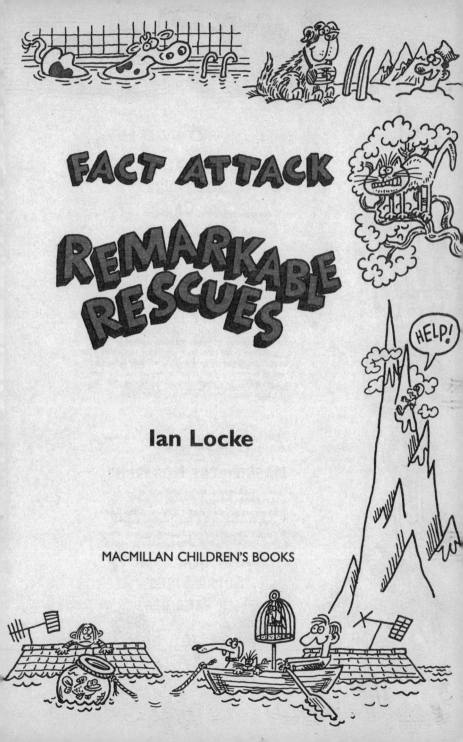

FACT ATTACK

REMARKABLE RESCUES

Ian Locke

MACMILLAN CHILDREN'S BOOKS

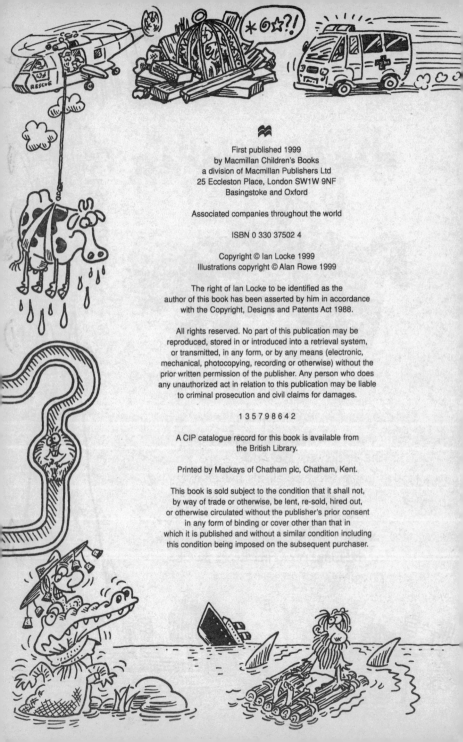

First published 1999
by Macmillan Children's Books
a division of Macmillan Publishers Ltd
25 Eccleston Place, London SW1W 9NF
Basingstoke and Oxford

Associated companies throughout the world

ISBN 0 330 37502 4

1 3 5 7 9 8 6 4 2

A CIP catalogue record for this book is available from
the British Library.

Printed by Mackays of Chatham plc, Chatham, Kent.

REMARKABLE RESCUES

DID YOU KNOW THAT ...

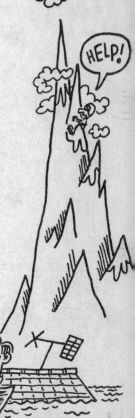

★ After a fancy dress party in Vienna in 1960, a British diplomat named Derek Davies found that his car, a Morris Minor, was covered in snow and that the locks on the door were frozen. Having used up all his matches trying to unfreeze the door, he tried blowing on the lock. His lips got stuck! He was rescued by two policemen and taken to hospital, still in his fancy dress costume.

5

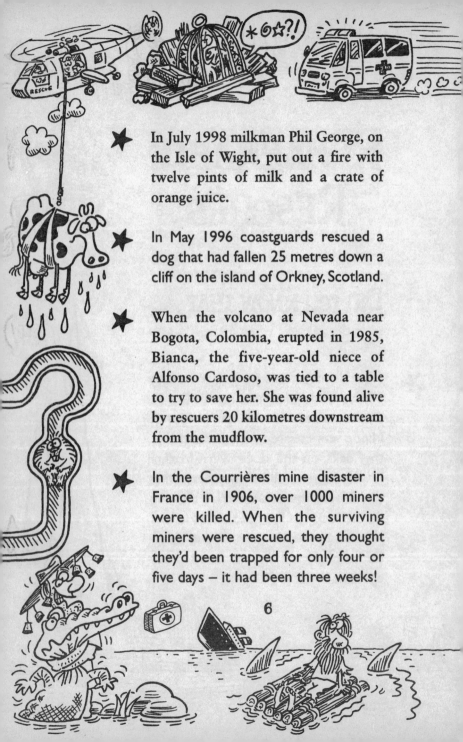

★ In July 1998 milkman Phil George, on the Isle of Wight, put out a fire with twelve pints of milk and a crate of orange juice.

★ In May 1996 coastguards rescued a dog that had fallen 25 metres down a cliff on the island of Orkney, Scotland.

★ When the volcano at Nevada near Bogota, Colombia, erupted in 1985, Bianca, the five-year-old niece of Alfonso Cardoso, was tied to a table to try to save her. She was found alive by rescuers 20 kilometres downstream from the mudflow.

★ In the Courrières mine disaster in France in 1906, over 1000 miners were killed. When the surviving miners were rescued, they thought they'd been trapped for only four or five days — it had been three weeks!

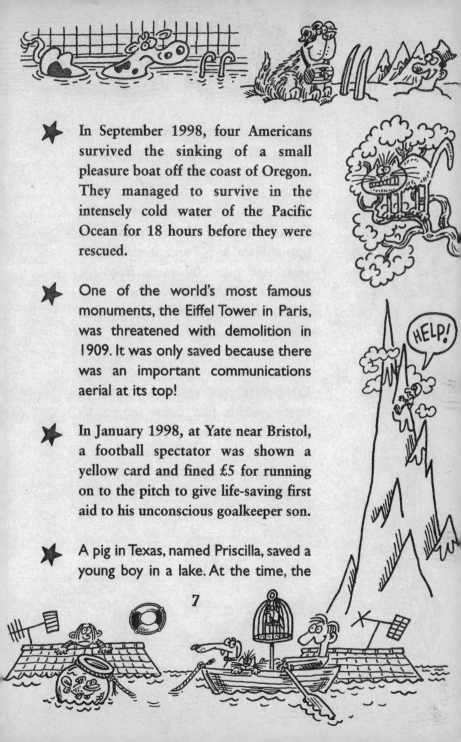

★ In September 1998, four Americans survived the sinking of a small pleasure boat off the coast of Oregon. They managed to survive in the intensely cold water of the Pacific Ocean for 18 hours before they were rescued.

★ One of the world's most famous monuments, the Eiffel Tower in Paris, was threatened with demolition in 1909. It was only saved because there was an important communications aerial at its top!

★ In January 1998, at Yate near Bristol, a football spectator was shown a yellow card and fined £5 for running on to the pitch to give life-saving first aid to his unconscious goalkeeper son.

★ A pig in Texas, named Priscilla, saved a young boy in a lake. At the time, the

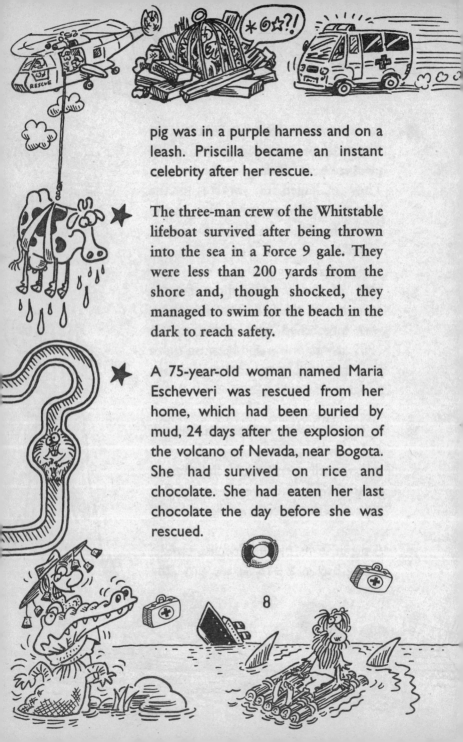

pig was in a purple harness and on a leash. Priscilla became an instant celebrity after her rescue.

The three-man crew of the Whitstable lifeboat survived after being thrown into the sea in a Force 9 gale. They were less than 200 yards from the shore and, though shocked, they managed to swim for the beach in the dark to reach safety.

A 75-year-old woman named Maria Eschevveri was rescued from her home, which had been buried by mud, 24 days after the explosion of the volcano of Nevada, near Bogota. She had survived on rice and chocolate. She had eaten her last chocolate the day before she was rescued.

8

★ The war dog school was set up in 1916 at Shoeburyness in Kent to train dogs for rescue missions.

★ One of the items stored for rescue in the event of a nuclear attack in the United States was the recipe for Wrigley's chewing gum.

★ Stuart Diver was found alive by rescuers at Thredbo, Australia, in an 'ice tomb' after the ski resort was hit by a landslide. Two chalets were demolished and he was trapped beneath concrete, mud and ice. His rescue was shown live on TV.

★ Fido, an eight-month-old rat, alerted a family in Torquay, Devon, to a fire in 1998. An electric heater had set fire to the carpet and furniture downstairs. Fido left his unfastened cage and climbed 15 stairs, each 20

9

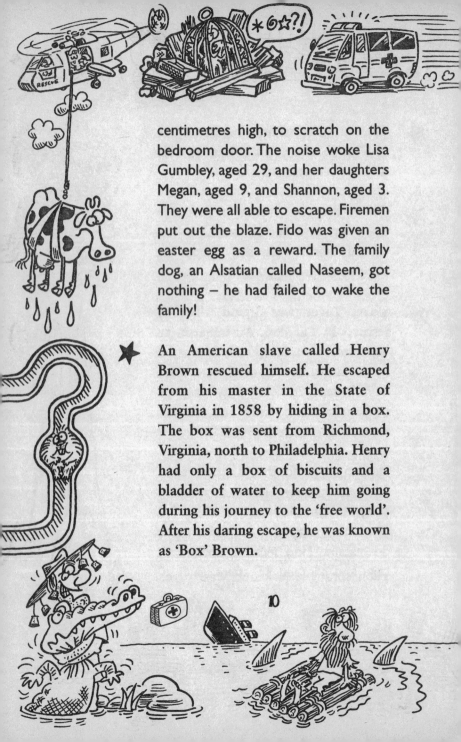

centimetres high, to scratch on the bedroom door. The noise woke Lisa Gumbley, aged 29, and her daughters Megan, aged 9, and Shannon, aged 3. They were all able to escape. Firemen put out the blaze. Fido was given an easter egg as a reward. The family dog, an Alsatian called Naseem, got nothing — he had failed to wake the family!

An American slave called Henry Brown rescued himself. He escaped from his master in the State of Virginia in 1858 by hiding in a box. The box was sent from Richmond, Virginia, north to Philadelphia. Henry had only a box of biscuits and a bladder of water to keep him going during his journey to the 'free world'. After his daring escape, he was known as 'Box' Brown.

10

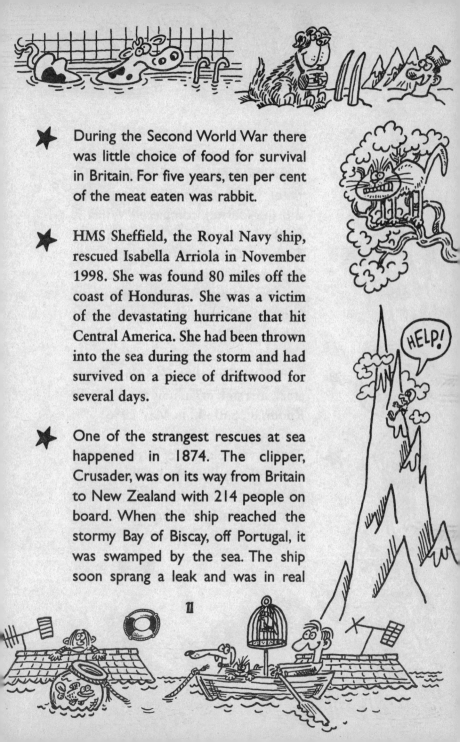

During the Second World War there was little choice of food for survival in Britain. For five years, ten per cent of the meat eaten was rabbit.

HMS Sheffield, the Royal Navy ship, rescued Isabella Arriola in November 1998. She was found 80 miles off the coast of Honduras. She was a victim of the devastating hurricane that hit Central America. She had been thrown into the sea during the storm and had survived on a piece of driftwood for several days.

One of the strangest rescues at sea happened in 1874. The clipper, Crusader, was on its way from Britain to New Zealand with 214 people on board. When the ship reached the stormy Bay of Biscay, off Portugal, it was swamped by the sea. The ship soon sprang a leak and was in real

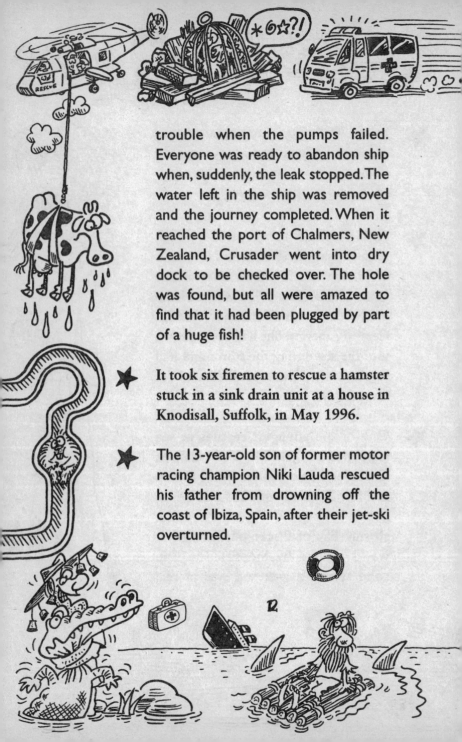

trouble when the pumps failed. Everyone was ready to abandon ship when, suddenly, the leak stopped. The water left in the ship was removed and the journey completed. When it reached the port of Chalmers, New Zealand, Crusader went into dry dock to be checked over. The hole was found, but all were amazed to find that it had been plugged by part of a huge fish!

★ It took six firemen to rescue a hamster stuck in a sink drain unit at a house in Knodisall, Suffolk, in May 1996.

★ The 13-year-old son of former motor racing champion Niki Lauda rescued his father from drowning off the coast of Ibiza, Spain, after their jet-ski overturned.

12

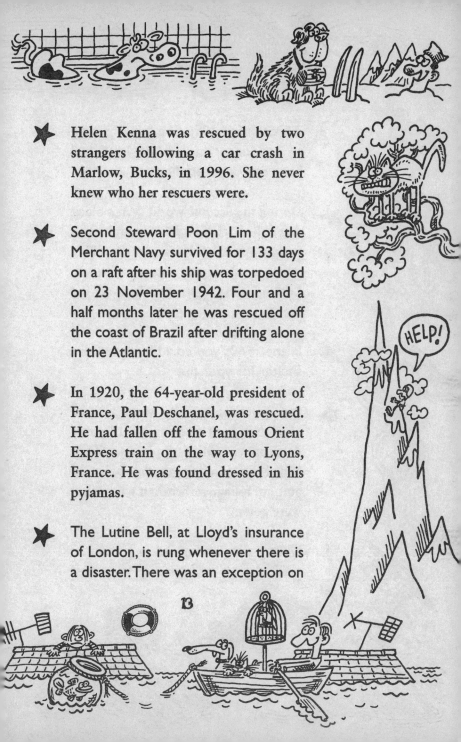

★ Helen Kenna was rescued by two strangers following a car crash in Marlow, Bucks, in 1996. She never knew who her rescuers were.

★ Second Steward Poon Lim of the Merchant Navy survived for 133 days on a raft after his ship was torpedoed on 23 November 1942. Four and a half months later he was rescued off the coast of Brazil after drifting alone in the Atlantic.

★ In 1920, the 64-year-old president of France, Paul Deschanel, was rescued. He had fallen off the famous Orient Express train on the way to Lyons, France. He was found dressed in his pyjamas.

★ The Lutine Bell, at Lloyd's insurance of London, is rung whenever there is a disaster. There was an exception on

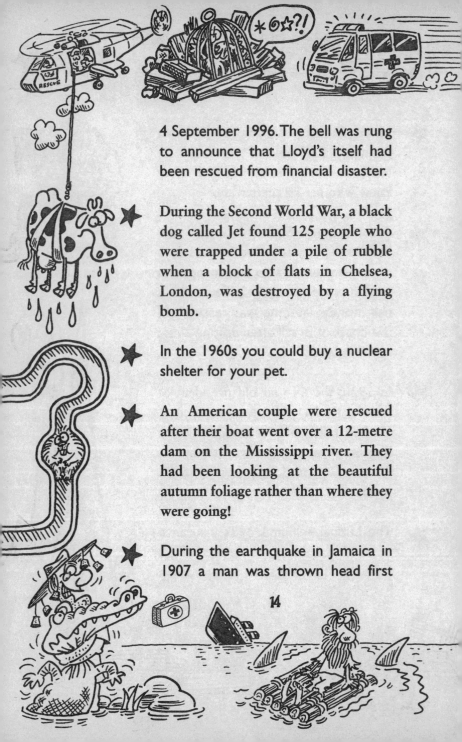

4 September 1996. The bell was rung to announce that Lloyd's itself had been rescued from financial disaster.

★ During the Second World War, a black dog called Jet found 125 people who were trapped under a pile of rubble when a block of flats in Chelsea, London, was destroyed by a flying bomb.

★ In the 1960s you could buy a nuclear shelter for your pet.

★ An American couple were rescued after their boat went over a 12-metre dam on the Mississippi river. They had been looking at the beautiful autumn foliage rather than where they were going!

★ During the earthquake in Jamaica in 1907 a man was thrown head first

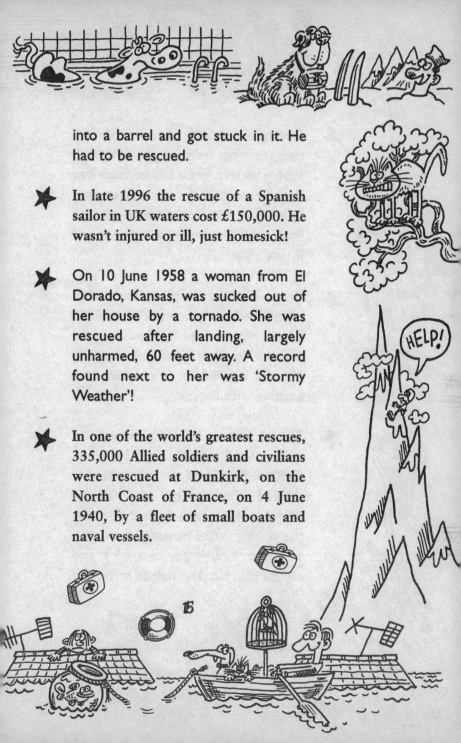

into a barrel and got stuck in it. He had to be rescued.

★ In late 1996 the rescue of a Spanish sailor in UK waters cost £150,000. He wasn't injured or ill, just homesick!

★ On 10 June 1958 a woman from El Dorado, Kansas, was sucked out of her house by a tornado. She was rescued after landing, largely unharmed, 60 feet away. A record found next to her was 'Stormy Weather'!

★ In one of the world's greatest rescues, 335,000 Allied soldiers and civilians were rescued at Dunkirk, on the North Coast of France, on 4 June 1940, by a fleet of small boats and naval vessels.

15

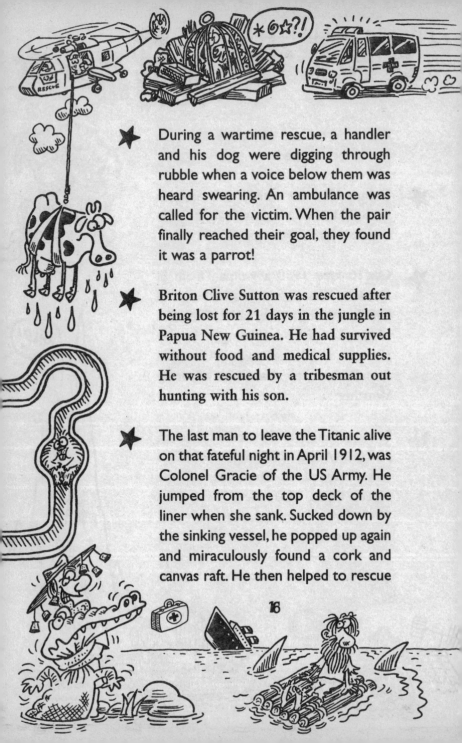

During a wartime rescue, a handler and his dog were digging through rubble when a voice below them was heard swearing. An ambulance was called for the victim. When the pair finally reached their goal, they found it was a parrot!

Briton Clive Sutton was rescued after being lost for 21 days in the jungle in Papua New Guinea. He had survived without food and medical supplies. He was rescued by a tribesman out hunting with his son.

The last man to leave the Titanic alive on that fateful night in April 1912, was Colonel Gracie of the US Army. He jumped from the top deck of the liner when she sank. Sucked down by the sinking vessel, he popped up again and miraculously found a cork and canvas raft. He then helped to rescue

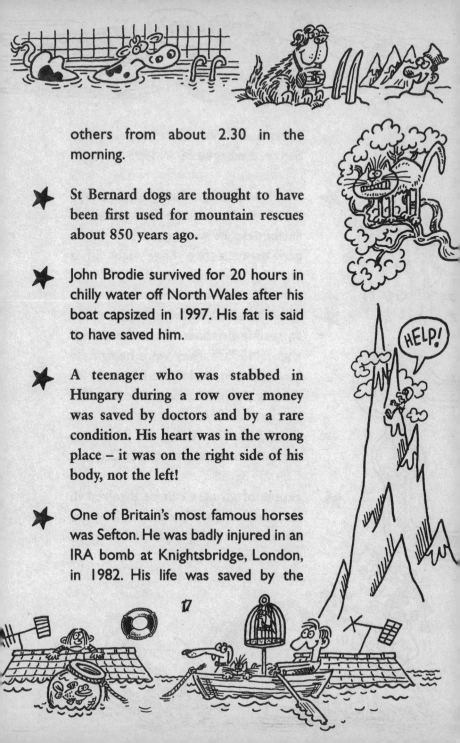

others from about 2.30 in the morning.

⭐ St Bernard dogs are thought to have been first used for mountain rescues about 850 years ago.

⭐ John Brodie survived for 20 hours in chilly water off North Wales after his boat capsized in 1997. His fat is said to have saved him.

⭐ A teenager who was stabbed in Hungary during a row over money was saved by doctors and by a rare condition. His heart was in the wrong place – it was on the right side of his body, not the left!

⭐ One of Britain's most famous horses was Sefton. He was badly injured in an IRA bomb at Knightsbridge, London, in 1982. His life was saved by the

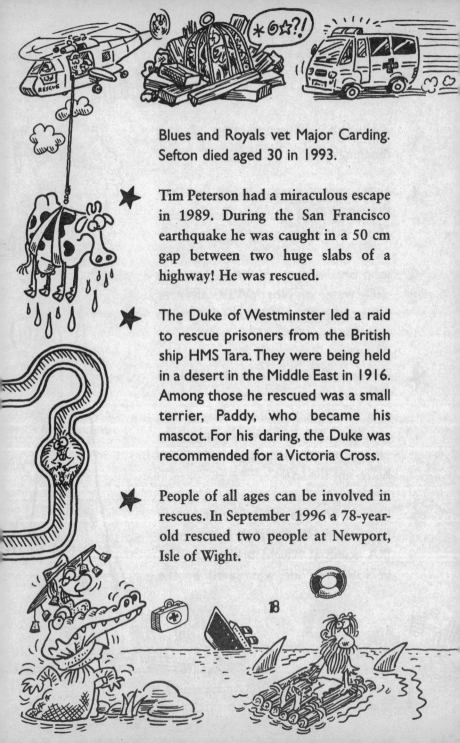

Blues and Royals vet Major Carding. Sefton died aged 30 in 1993.

Tim Peterson had a miraculous escape in 1989. During the San Francisco earthquake he was caught in a 50 cm gap between two huge slabs of a highway! He was rescued.

The Duke of Westminster led a raid to rescue prisoners from the British ship HMS Tara. They were being held in a desert in the Middle East in 1916. Among those he rescued was a small terrier, Paddy, who became his mascot. For his daring, the Duke was recommended for a Victoria Cross.

People of all ages can be involved in rescues. In September 1996 a 78-year-old rescued two people at Newport, Isle of Wight.

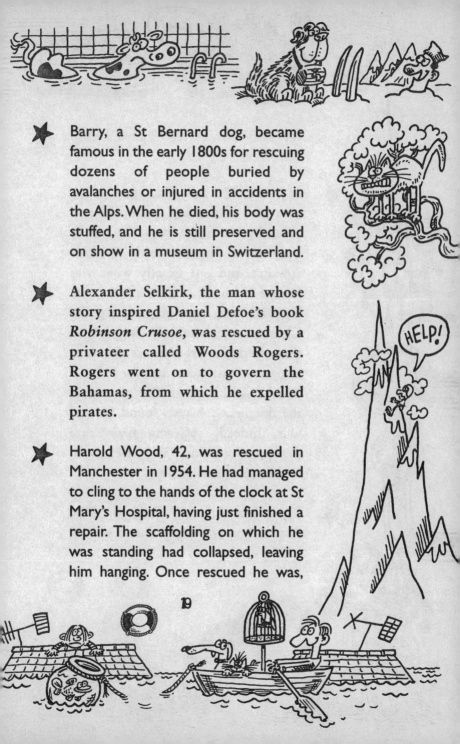

★ Barry, a St Bernard dog, became famous in the early 1800s for rescuing dozens of people buried by avalanches or injured in accidents in the Alps. When he died, his body was stuffed, and he is still preserved and on show in a museum in Switzerland.

★ Alexander Selkirk, the man whose story inspired Daniel Defoe's book *Robinson Crusoe*, was rescued by a privateer called Woods Rogers. Rogers went on to govern the Bahamas, from which he expelled pirates.

★ Harold Wood, 42, was rescued in Manchester in 1954. He had managed to cling to the hands of the clock at St Mary's Hospital, having just finished a repair. The scaffolding on which he was standing had collapsed, leaving him hanging. Once rescued he was,

HELP!

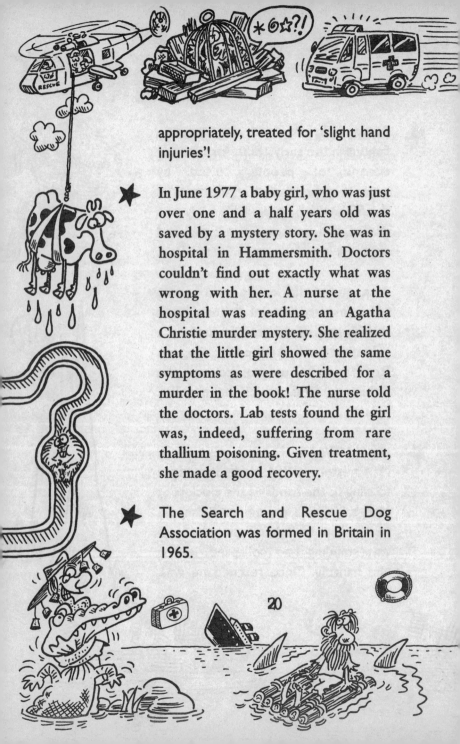

appropriately, treated for 'slight hand injuries'!

★ In June 1977 a baby girl, who was just over one and a half years old was saved by a mystery story. She was in hospital in Hammersmith. Doctors couldn't find out exactly what was wrong with her. A nurse at the hospital was reading an Agatha Christie murder mystery. She realized that the little girl showed the same symptoms as were described for a murder in the book! The nurse told the doctors. Lab tests found the girl was, indeed, suffering from rare thallium poisoning. Given treatment, she made a good recovery.

★ The Search and Rescue Dog Association was formed in Britain in 1965.

20

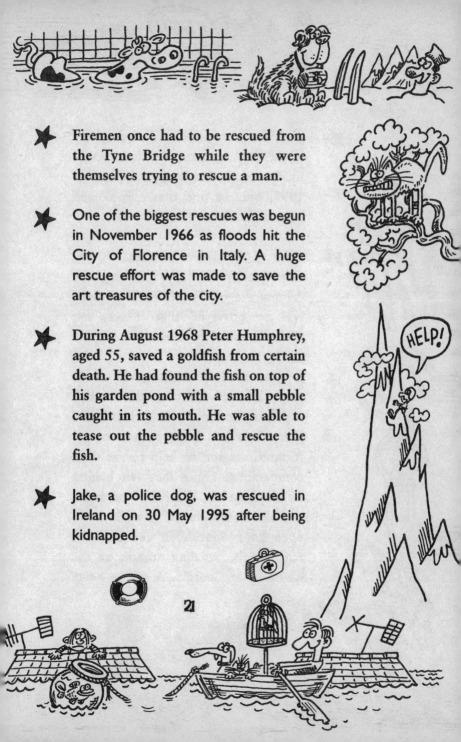

★ Firemen once had to be rescued from the Tyne Bridge while they were themselves trying to rescue a man.

★ One of the biggest rescues was begun in November 1966 as floods hit the City of Florence in Italy. A huge rescue effort was made to save the art treasures of the city.

★ During August 1968 Peter Humphrey, aged 55, saved a goldfish from certain death. He had found the fish on top of his garden pond with a small pebble caught in its mouth. He was able to tease out the pebble and rescue the fish.

★ Jake, a police dog, was rescued in Ireland on 30 May 1995 after being kidnapped.

HELP!

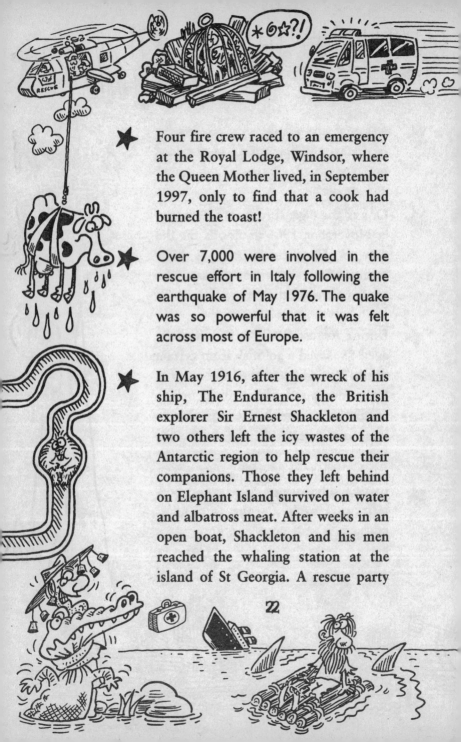

Four fire crew raced to an emergency at the Royal Lodge, Windsor, where the Queen Mother lived, in September 1997, only to find that a cook had burned the toast!

Over 7,000 were involved in the rescue effort in Italy following the earthquake of May 1976. The quake was so powerful that it was felt across most of Europe.

In May 1916, after the wreck of his ship, The Endurance, the British explorer Sir Ernest Shackleton and two others left the icy wastes of the Antarctic region to help rescue their companions. Those they left behind on Elephant Island survived on water and albatross meat. After weeks in an open boat, Shackleton and his men reached the whaling station at the island of St Georgia. A rescue party

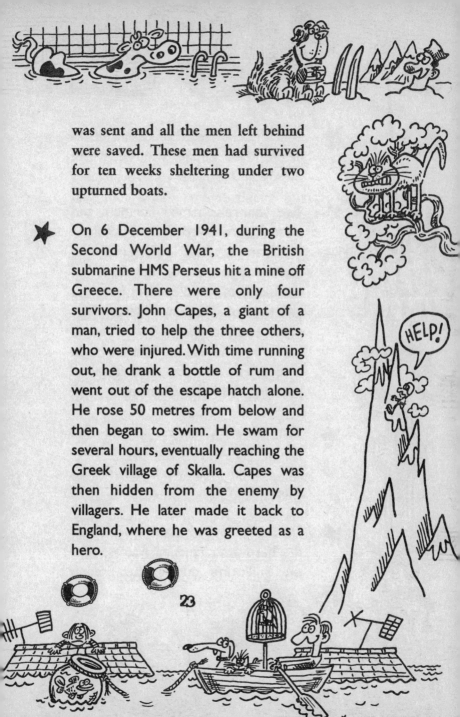

was sent and all the men left behind were saved. These men had survived for ten weeks sheltering under two upturned boats.

★ On 6 December 1941, during the Second World War, the British submarine HMS Perseus hit a mine off Greece. There were only four survivors. John Capes, a giant of a man, tried to help the three others, who were injured. With time running out, he drank a bottle of rum and went out of the escape hatch alone. He rose 50 metres from below and then began to swim. He swam for several hours, eventually reaching the Greek village of Skalla. Capes was then hidden from the enemy by villagers. He later made it back to England, where he was greeted as a hero.

23

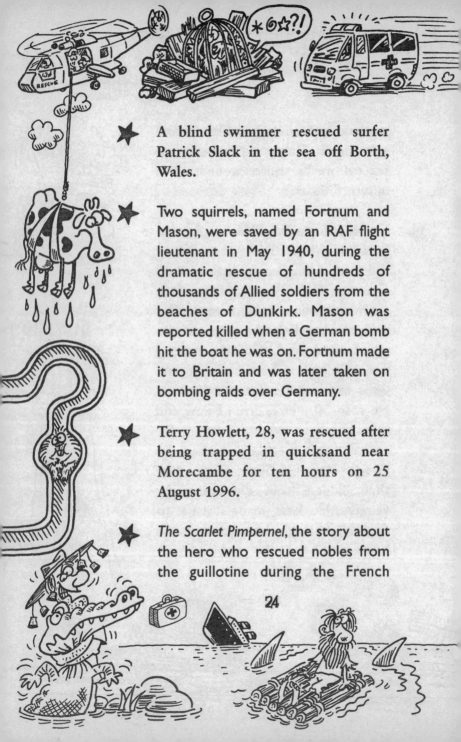

A blind swimmer rescued surfer Patrick Slack in the sea off Borth, Wales.

Two squirrels, named Fortnum and Mason, were saved by an RAF flight lieutenant in May 1940, during the dramatic rescue of hundreds of thousands of Allied soldiers from the beaches of Dunkirk. Mason was reported killed when a German bomb hit the boat he was on. Fortnum made it to Britain and was later taken on bombing raids over Germany.

Terry Howlett, 28, was rescued after being trapped in quicksand near Morecambe for ten hours on 25 August 1996.

The Scarlet Pimpernel, the story about the hero who rescued nobles from the guillotine during the French

24

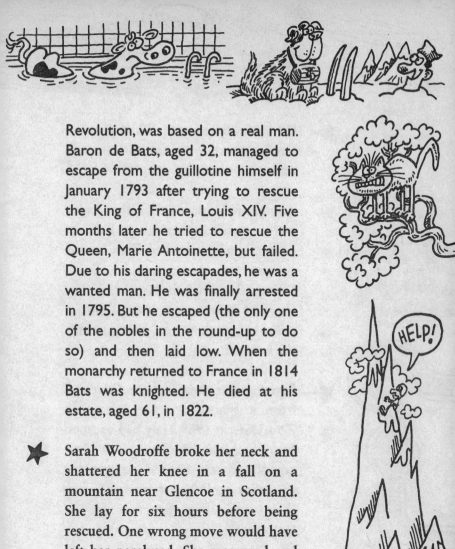

Revolution, was based on a real man. Baron de Bats, aged 32, managed to escape from the guillotine himself in January 1793 after trying to rescue the King of France, Louis XIV. Five months later he tried to rescue the Queen, Marie Antoinette, but failed. Due to his daring escapades, he was a wanted man. He was finally arrested in 1795. But he escaped (the only one of the nobles in the round-up to do so) and then laid low. When the monarchy returned to France in 1814 Bats was knighted. He died at his estate, aged 61, in 1822.

★ Sarah Woodroffe broke her neck and shattered her knee in a fall on a mountain near Glencoe in Scotland. She lay for six hours before being rescued. One wrong move would have left her paralysed. She recovered and was soon back on her feet.

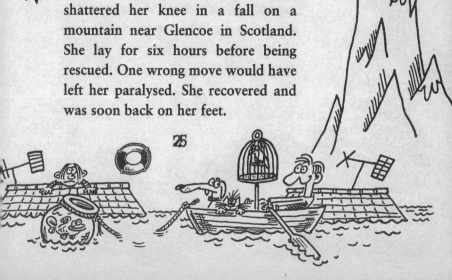

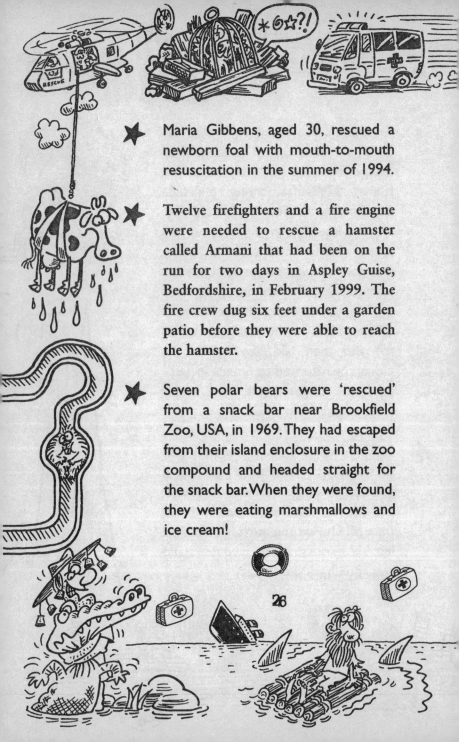

★ Maria Gibbens, aged 30, rescued a newborn foal with mouth-to-mouth resuscitation in the summer of 1994.

★ Twelve firefighters and a fire engine were needed to rescue a hamster called Armani that had been on the run for two days in Aspley Guise, Bedfordshire, in February 1999. The fire crew dug six feet under a garden patio before they were able to reach the hamster.

★ Seven polar bears were 'rescued' from a snack bar near Brookfield Zoo, USA, in 1969. They had escaped from their island enclosure in the zoo compound and headed straight for the snack bar. When they were found, they were eating marshmallows and ice cream!

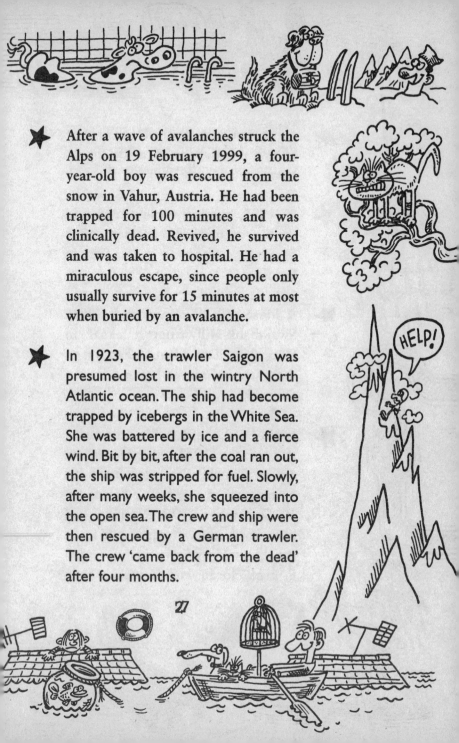

After a wave of avalanches struck the Alps on 19 February 1999, a four-year-old boy was rescued from the snow in Vahur, Austria. He had been trapped for 100 minutes and was clinically dead. Revived, he survived and was taken to hospital. He had a miraculous escape, since people only usually survive for 15 minutes at most when buried by an avalanche.

In 1923, the trawler Saigon was presumed lost in the wintry North Atlantic ocean. The ship had become trapped by icebergs in the White Sea. She was battered by ice and a fierce wind. Bit by bit, after the coal ran out, the ship was stripped for fuel. Slowly, after many weeks, she squeezed into the open sea. The crew and ship were then rescued by a German trawler. The crew 'came back from the dead' after four months.

HELP!

27

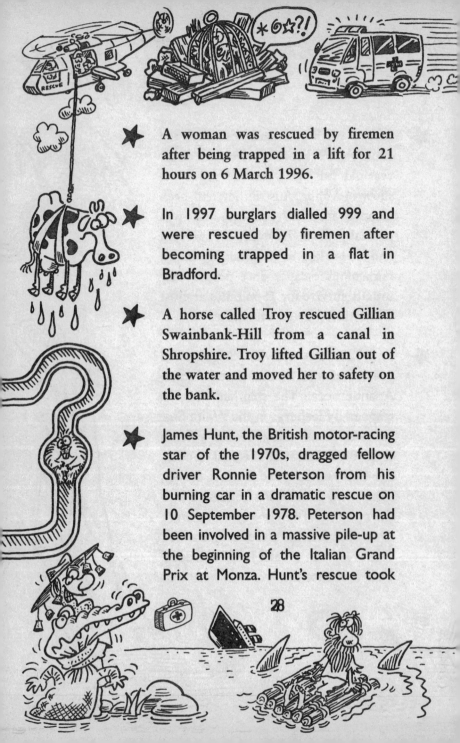

A woman was rescued by firemen after being trapped in a lift for 21 hours on 6 March 1996.

In 1997 burglars dialled 999 and were rescued by firemen after becoming trapped in a flat in Bradford.

A horse called Troy rescued Gillian Swainbank-Hill from a canal in Shropshire. Troy lifted Gillian out of the water and moved her to safety on the bank.

James Hunt, the British motor-racing star of the 1970s, dragged fellow driver Ronnie Peterson from his burning car in a dramatic rescue on 10 September 1978. Peterson had been involved in a massive pile-up at the beginning of the Italian Grand Prix at Monza. Hunt's rescue took

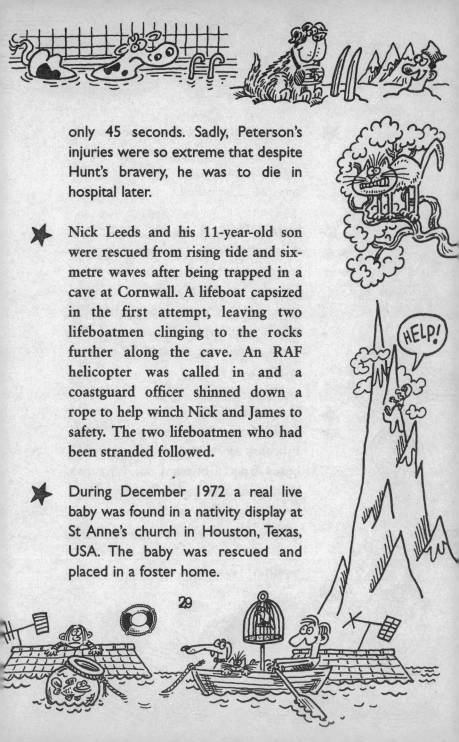

only 45 seconds. Sadly, Peterson's injuries were so extreme that despite Hunt's bravery, he was to die in hospital later.

⭐ Nick Leeds and his 11-year-old son were rescued from rising tide and six-metre waves after being trapped in a cave at Cornwall. A lifeboat capsized in the first attempt, leaving two lifeboatmen clinging to the rocks further along the cave. An RAF helicopter was called in and a coastguard officer shinned down a rope to help winch Nick and James to safety. The two lifeboatmen who had been stranded followed.

⭐ During December 1972 a real live baby was found in a nativity display at St Anne's church in Houston, Texas, USA. The baby was rescued and placed in a foster home.

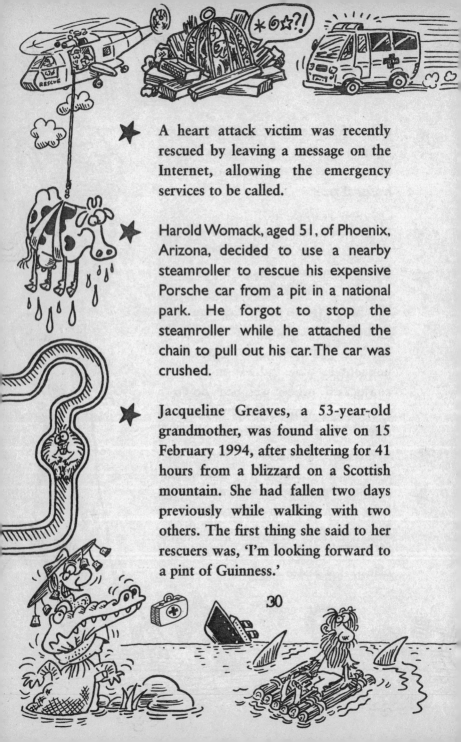

★ A heart attack victim was recently rescued by leaving a message on the Internet, allowing the emergency services to be called.

★ Harold Womack, aged 51, of Phoenix, Arizona, decided to use a nearby steamroller to rescue his expensive Porsche car from a pit in a national park. He forgot to stop the steamroller while he attached the chain to pull out his car. The car was crushed.

★ Jacqueline Greaves, a 53-year-old grandmother, was found alive on 15 February 1994, after sheltering for 41 hours from a blizzard on a Scottish mountain. She had fallen two days previously while walking with two others. The first thing she said to her rescuers was, 'I'm looking forward to a pint of Guinness.'

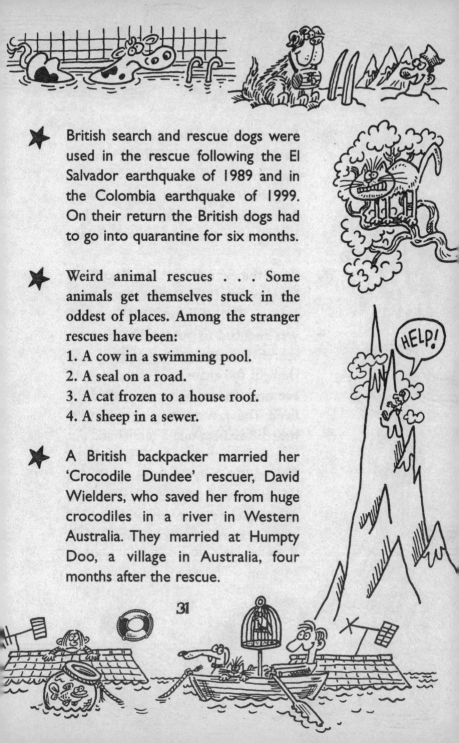

British search and rescue dogs were used in the rescue following the El Salvador earthquake of 1989 and in the Colombia earthquake of 1999. On their return the British dogs had to go into quarantine for six months.

Weird animal rescues . . . Some animals get themselves stuck in the oddest of places. Among the stranger rescues have been:
1. A cow in a swimming pool.
2. A seal on a road.
3. A cat frozen to a house roof.
4. A sheep in a sewer.

A British backpacker married her 'Crocodile Dundee' rescuer, David Wielders, who saved her from huge crocodiles in a river in Western Australia. They married at Humpty Doo, a village in Australia, four months after the rescue.

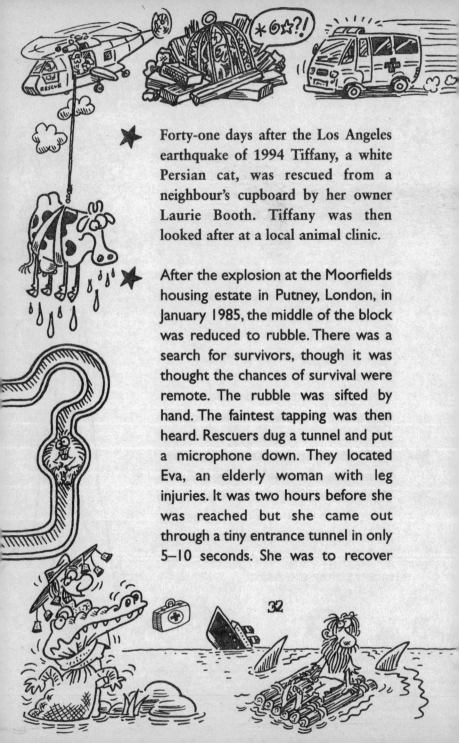

Forty-one days after the Los Angeles earthquake of 1994 Tiffany, a white Persian cat, was rescued from a neighbour's cupboard by her owner Laurie Booth. Tiffany was then looked after at a local animal clinic.

After the explosion at the Moorfields housing estate in Putney, London, in January 1985, the middle of the block was reduced to rubble. There was a search for survivors, though it was thought the chances of survival were remote. The rubble was sifted by hand. The faintest tapping was then heard. Rescuers dug a tunnel and put a microphone down. They located Eva, an elderly woman with leg injuries. It was two hours before she was reached but she came out through a tiny entrance tunnel in only 5–10 seconds. She was to recover

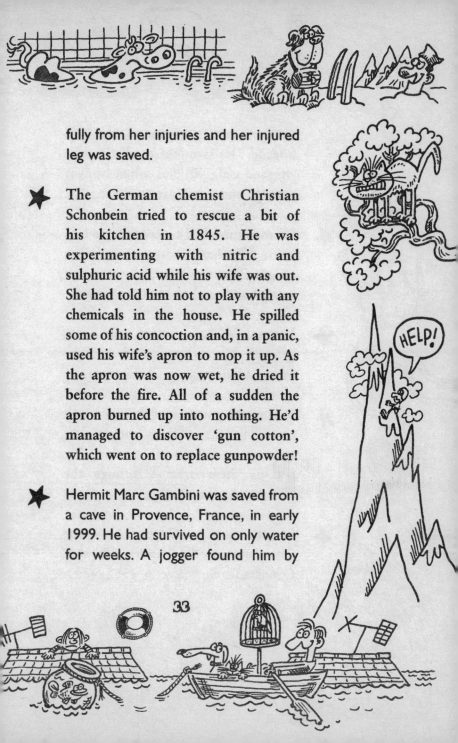

fully from her injuries and her injured leg was saved.

★ The German chemist Christian Schonbein tried to rescue a bit of his kitchen in 1845. He was experimenting with nitric and sulphuric acid while his wife was out. She had told him not to play with any chemicals in the house. He spilled some of his concoction and, in a panic, used his wife's apron to mop it up. As the apron was now wet, he dried it before the fire. All of a sudden the apron burned up into nothing. He'd managed to discover 'gun cotton', which went on to replace gunpowder!

★ Hermit Marc Gambini was saved from a cave in Provence, France, in early 1999. He had survived on only water for weeks. A jogger found him by

33

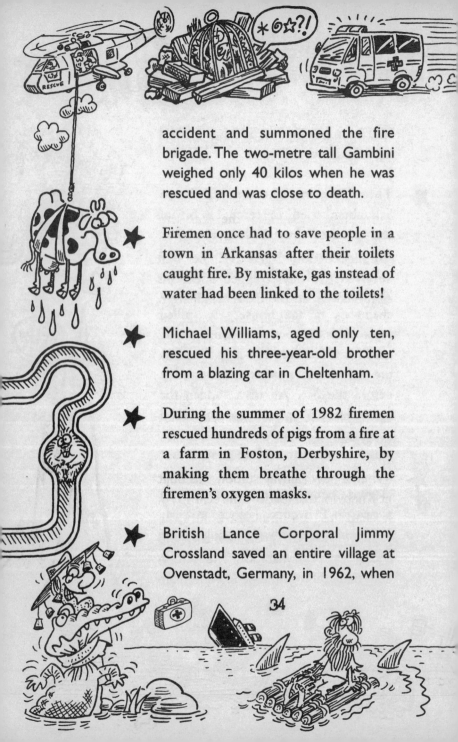

accident and summoned the fire brigade. The two-metre tall Gambini weighed only 40 kilos when he was rescued and was close to death.

★ Firemen once had to save people in a town in Arkansas after their toilets caught fire. By mistake, gas instead of water had been linked to the toilets!

★ Michael Williams, aged only ten, rescued his three-year-old brother from a blazing car in Cheltenham.

★ During the summer of 1982 firemen rescued hundreds of pigs from a fire at a farm in Foston, Derbyshire, by making them breathe through the firemen's oxygen masks.

★ British Lance Corporal Jimmy Crossland saved an entire village at Ovenstadt, Germany, in 1962, when

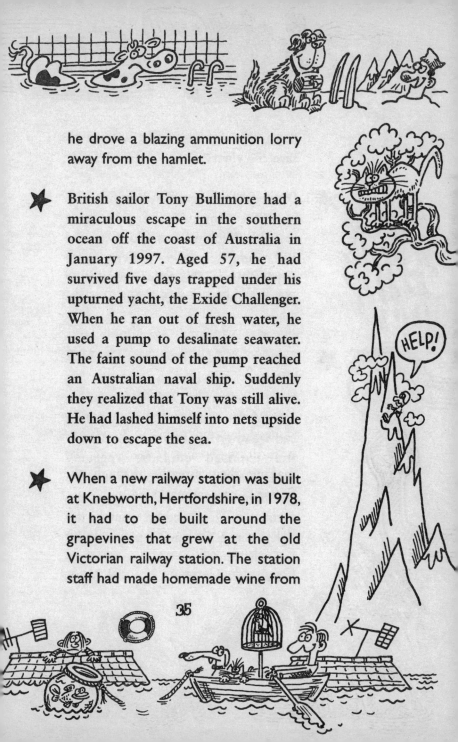

he drove a blazing ammunition lorry away from the hamlet.

★ British sailor Tony Bullimore had a miraculous escape in the southern ocean off the coast of Australia in January 1997. Aged 57, he had survived five days trapped under his upturned yacht, the Exide Challenger. When he ran out of fresh water, he used a pump to desalinate seawater. The faint sound of the pump reached an Australian naval ship. Suddenly they realized that Tony was still alive. He had lashed himself into nets upside down to escape the sea.

★ When a new railway station was built at Knebworth, Hertfordshire, in 1978, it had to be built around the grapevines that grew at the old Victorian railway station. The station staff had made homemade wine from

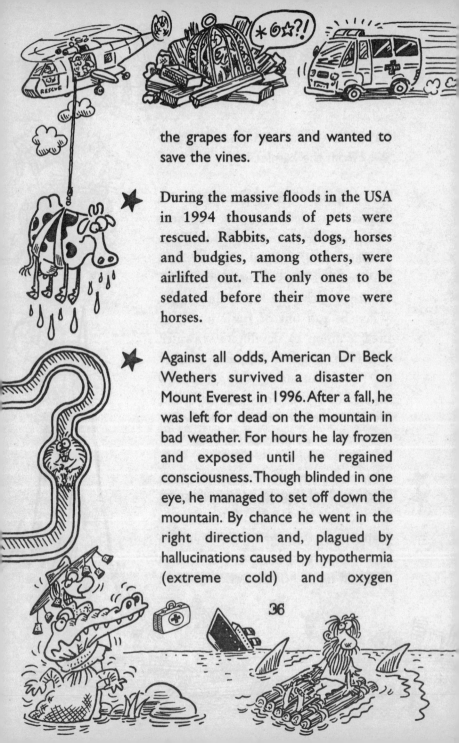

the grapes for years and wanted to save the vines.

★ During the massive floods in the USA in 1994 thousands of pets were rescued. Rabbits, cats, dogs, horses and budgies, among others, were airlifted out. The only ones to be sedated before their move were horses.

★ Against all odds, American Dr Beck Wethers survived a disaster on Mount Everest in 1996. After a fall, he was left for dead on the mountain in bad weather. For hours he lay frozen and exposed until he regained consciousness. Though blinded in one eye, he managed to set off down the mountain. By chance he went in the right direction and, plagued by hallucinations caused by hypothermia (extreme cold) and oxygen

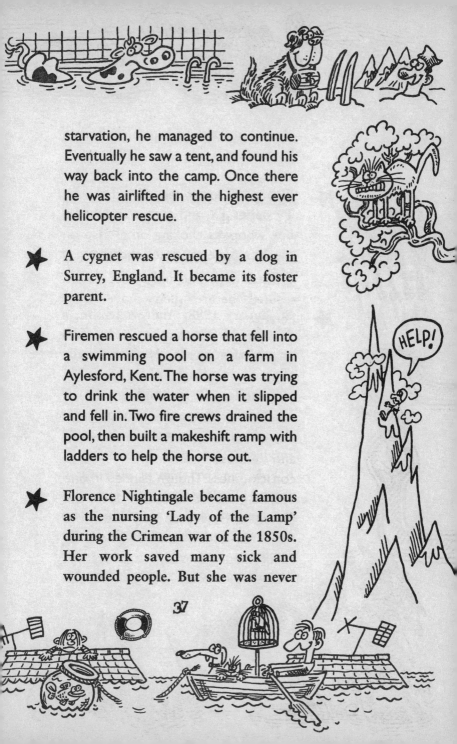

starvation, he managed to continue. Eventually he saw a tent, and found his way back into the camp. Once there he was airlifted in the highest ever helicopter rescue.

★ A cygnet was rescued by a dog in Surrey, England. It became its foster parent.

★ Firemen rescued a horse that fell into a swimming pool on a farm in Aylesford, Kent. The horse was trying to drink the water when it slipped and fell in. Two fire crews drained the pool, then built a makeshift ramp with ladders to help the horse out.

★ Florence Nightingale became famous as the nursing 'Lady of the Lamp' during the Crimean war of the 1850s. Her work saved many sick and wounded people. But she was never

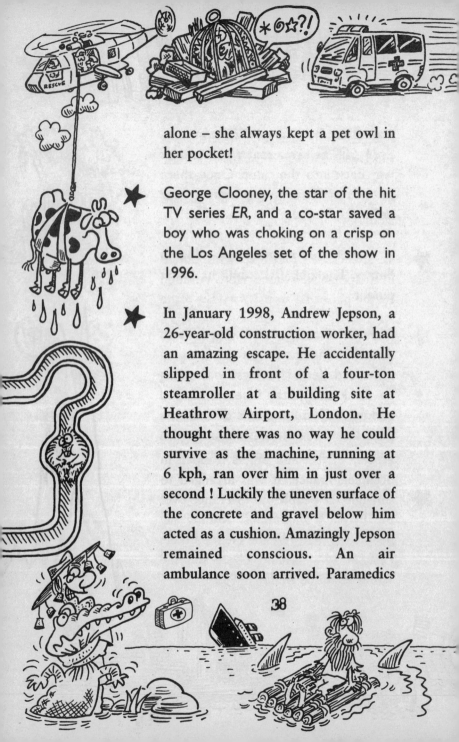

alone – she always kept a pet owl in her pocket!

★ George Clooney, the star of the hit TV series *ER*, and a co-star saved a boy who was choking on a crisp on the Los Angeles set of the show in 1996.

★ In January 1998, Andrew Jepson, a 26-year-old construction worker, had an amazing escape. He accidentally slipped in front of a four-ton steamroller at a building site at Heathrow Airport, London. He thought there was no way he could survive as the machine, running at 6 kph, ran over him in just over a second ! Luckily the uneven surface of the concrete and gravel below him acted as a cushion. Amazingly Jepson remained conscious. An air ambulance soon arrived. Paramedics

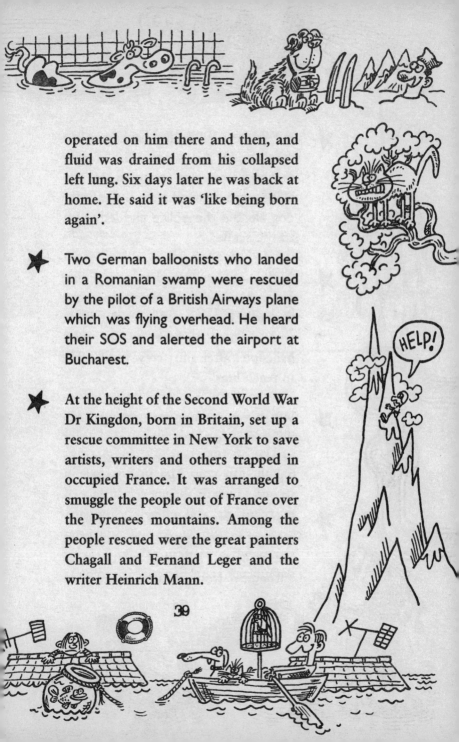

operated on him there and then, and fluid was drained from his collapsed left lung. Six days later he was back at home. He said it was 'like being born again'.

★ Two German balloonists who landed in a Romanian swamp were rescued by the pilot of a British Airways plane which was flying overhead. He heard their SOS and alerted the airport at Bucharest.

★ At the height of the Second World War Dr Kingdon, born in Britain, set up a rescue committee in New York to save artists, writers and others trapped in occupied France. It was arranged to smuggle the people out of France over the Pyrenees mountains. Among the people rescued were the great painters Chagall and Fernand Leger and the writer Heinrich Mann.

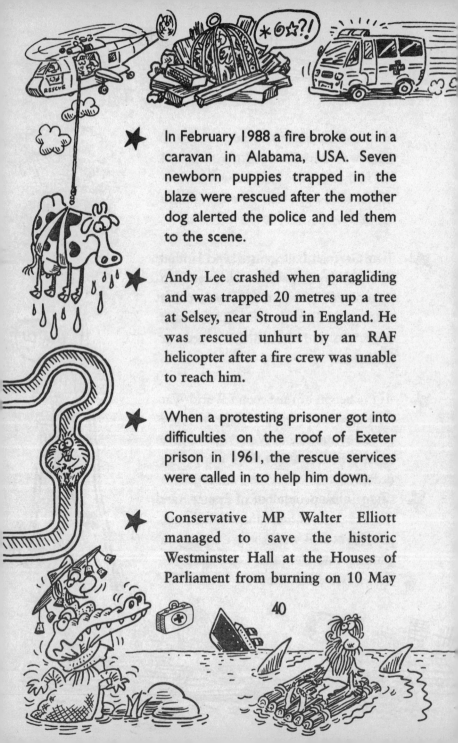

In February 1988 a fire broke out in a caravan in Alabama, USA. Seven newborn puppies trapped in the blaze were rescued after the mother dog alerted the police and led them to the scene.

Andy Lee crashed when paragliding and was trapped 20 metres up a tree at Selsey, near Stroud in England. He was rescued unhurt by an RAF helicopter after a fire crew was unable to reach him.

When a protesting prisoner got into difficulties on the roof of Exeter prison in 1961, the rescue services were called in to help him down.

Conservative MP Walter Elliott managed to save the historic Westminster Hall at the Houses of Parliament from burning on 10 May

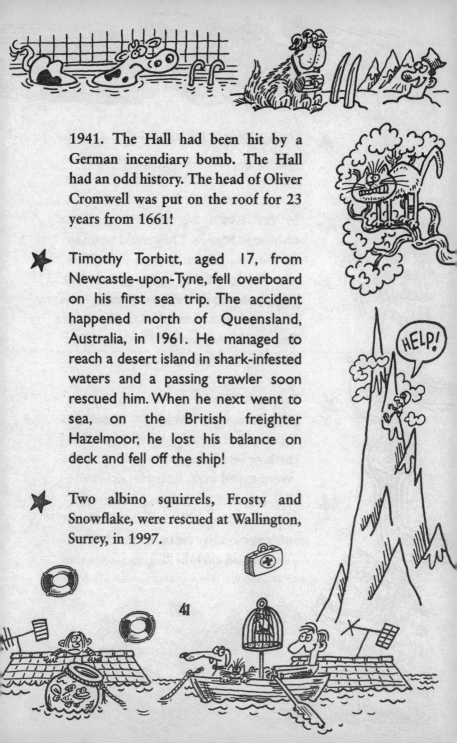

1941. The Hall had been hit by a German incendiary bomb. The Hall had an odd history. The head of Oliver Cromwell was put on the roof for 23 years from 1661!

⭐ Timothy Torbitt, aged 17, from Newcastle-upon-Tyne, fell overboard on his first sea trip. The accident happened north of Queensland, Australia, in 1961. He managed to reach a desert island in shark-infested waters and a passing trawler soon rescued him. When he next went to sea, on the British freighter Hazelmoor, he lost his balance on deck and fell off the ship!

⭐ Two albino squirrels, Frosty and Snowflake, were rescued at Wallington, Surrey, in 1997.

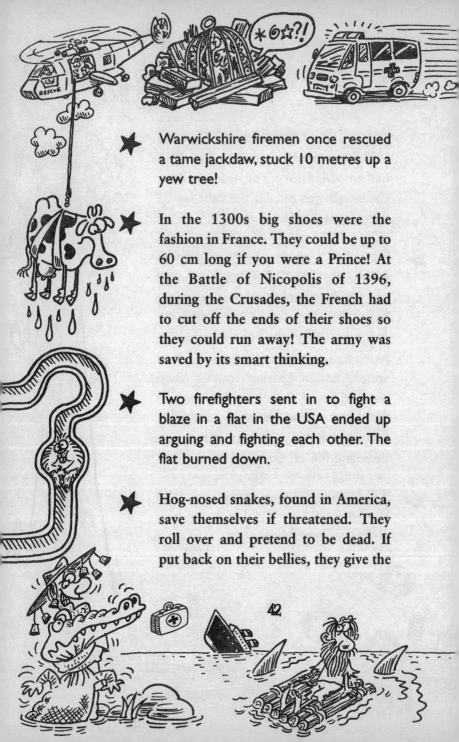

★ Warwickshire firemen once rescued a tame jackdaw, stuck 10 metres up a yew tree!

★ In the 1300s big shoes were the fashion in France. They could be up to 60 cm long if you were a Prince! At the Battle of Nicopolis of 1396, during the Crusades, the French had to cut off the ends of their shoes so they could run away! The army was saved by its smart thinking.

★ Two firefighters sent in to fight a blaze in a flat in the USA ended up arguing and fighting each other. The flat burned down.

★ Hog-nosed snakes, found in America, save themselves if threatened. They roll over and pretend to be dead. If put back on their bellies, they give the

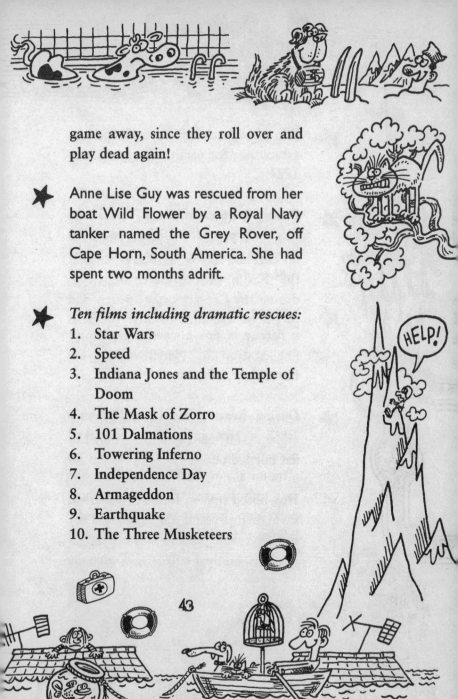

game away, since they roll over and play dead again!

⭐ Anne Lise Guy was rescued from her boat Wild Flower by a Royal Navy tanker named the Grey Rover, off Cape Horn, South America. She had spent two months adrift.

⭐ *Ten films including dramatic rescues:*
1. Star Wars
2. Speed
3. Indiana Jones and the Temple of Doom
4. The Mask of Zorro
5. 101 Dalmations
6. Towering Inferno
7. Independence Day
8. Armageddon
9. Earthquake
10. The Three Musketeers

HELP!

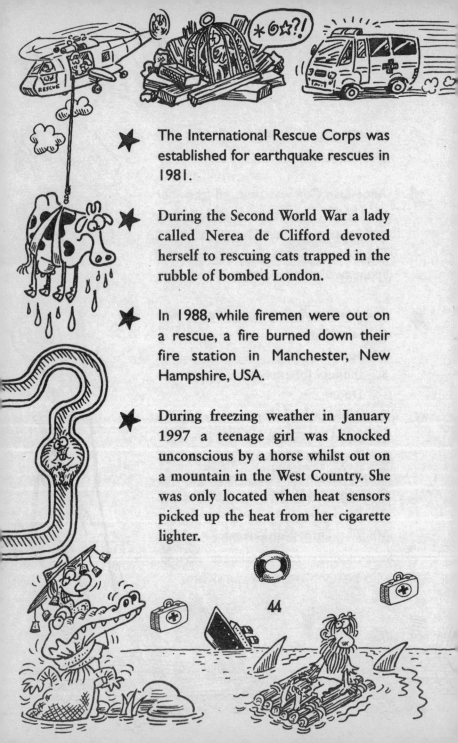

★ The International Rescue Corps was established for earthquake rescues in 1981.

★ During the Second World War a lady called Nerea de Clifford devoted herself to rescuing cats trapped in the rubble of bombed London.

★ In 1988, while firemen were out on a rescue, a fire burned down their fire station in Manchester, New Hampshire, USA.

★ During freezing weather in January 1997 a teenage girl was knocked unconscious by a horse whilst out on a mountain in the West Country. She was only located when heat sensors picked up the heat from her cigarette lighter.

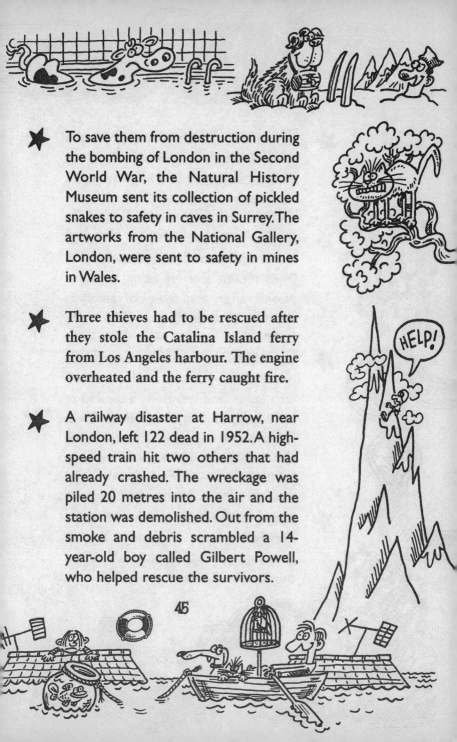

★ To save them from destruction during the bombing of London in the Second World War, the Natural History Museum sent its collection of pickled snakes to safety in caves in Surrey. The artworks from the National Gallery, London, were sent to safety in mines in Wales.

★ Three thieves had to be rescued after they stole the Catalina Island ferry from Los Angeles harbour. The engine overheated and the ferry caught fire.

★ A railway disaster at Harrow, near London, left 122 dead in 1952. A high-speed train hit two others that had already crashed. The wreckage was piled 20 metres into the air and the station was demolished. Out from the smoke and debris scrambled a 14-year-old boy called Gilbert Powell, who helped rescue the survivors.

HELP!

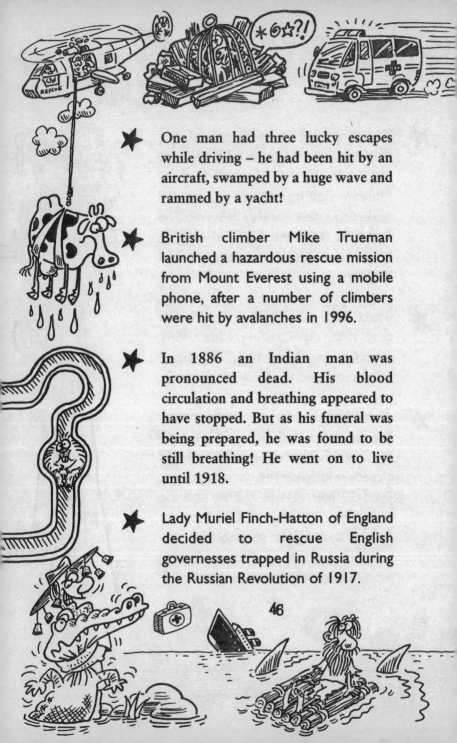

One man had three lucky escapes while driving – he had been hit by an aircraft, swamped by a huge wave and rammed by a yacht!

British climber Mike Trueman launched a hazardous rescue mission from Mount Everest using a mobile phone, after a number of climbers were hit by avalanches in 1996.

In 1886 an Indian man was pronounced dead. His blood circulation and breathing appeared to have stopped. But as his funeral was being prepared, he was found to be still breathing! He went on to live until 1918.

Lady Muriel Finch-Hatton of England decided to rescue English governesses trapped in Russia during the Russian Revolution of 1917.

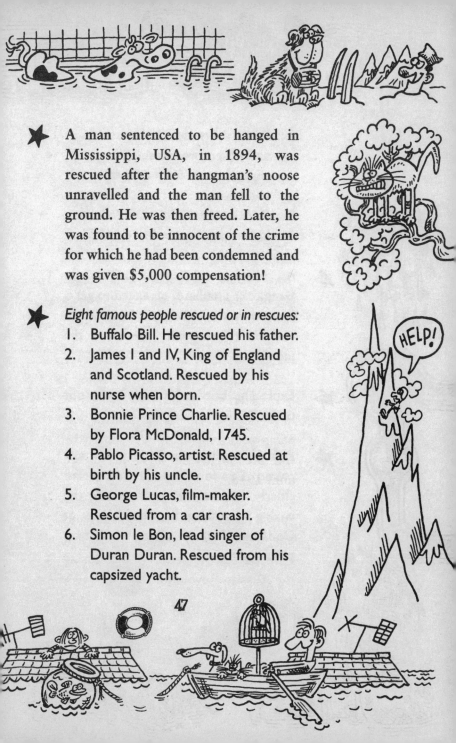

★ A man sentenced to be hanged in Mississippi, USA, in 1894, was rescued after the hangman's noose unravelled and the man fell to the ground. He was then freed. Later, he was found to be innocent of the crime for which he had been condemned and was given $5,000 compensation!

★ *Eight famous people rescued or in rescues:*
1. Buffalo Bill. He rescued his father.
2. James I and IV, King of England and Scotland. Rescued by his nurse when born.
3. Bonnie Prince Charlie. Rescued by Flora McDonald, 1745.
4. Pablo Picasso, artist. Rescued at birth by his uncle.
5. George Lucas, film-maker. Rescued from a car crash.
6. Simon le Bon, lead singer of Duran Duran. Rescued from his capsized yacht.

47

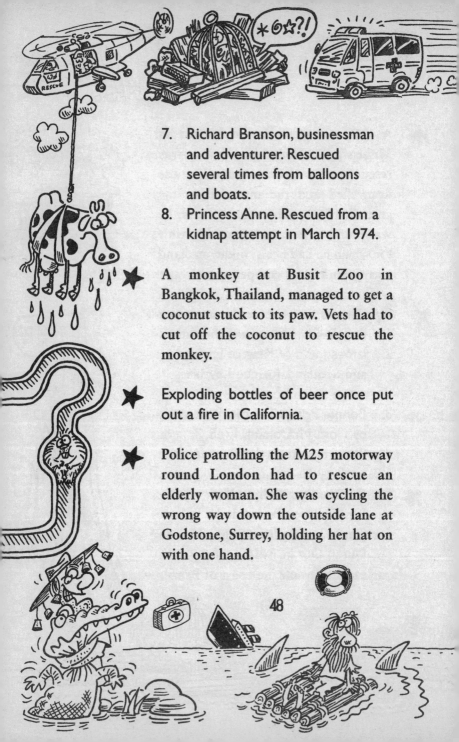

7. Richard Branson, businessman and adventurer. Rescued several times from balloons and boats.

8. Princess Anne. Rescued from a kidnap attempt in March 1974.

★ A monkey at Busit Zoo in Bangkok, Thailand, managed to get a coconut stuck to its paw. Vets had to cut off the coconut to rescue the monkey.

★ Exploding bottles of beer once put out a fire in California.

★ Police patrolling the M25 motorway round London had to rescue an elderly woman. She was cycling the wrong way down the outside lane at Godstone, Surrey, holding her hat on with one hand.

48

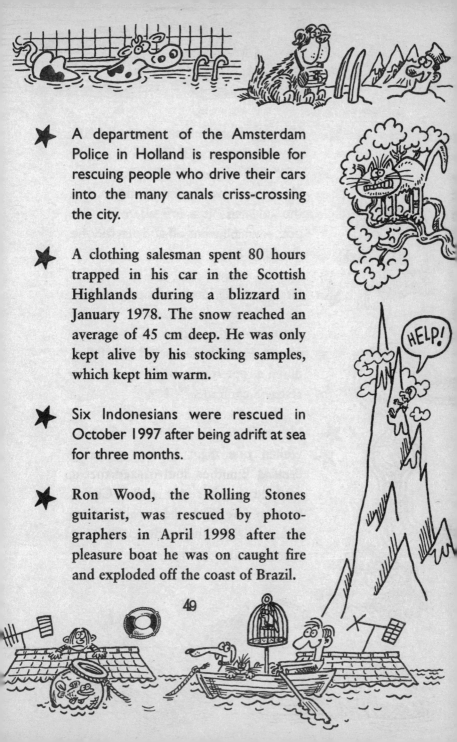

★ A department of the Amsterdam Police in Holland is responsible for rescuing people who drive their cars into the many canals criss-crossing the city.

★ A clothing salesman spent 80 hours trapped in his car in the Scottish Highlands during a blizzard in January 1978. The snow reached an average of 45 cm deep. He was only kept alive by his stocking samples, which kept him warm.

★ Six Indonesians were rescued in October 1997 after being adrift at sea for three months.

★ Ron Wood, the Rolling Stones guitarist, was rescued by photographers in April 1998 after the pleasure boat he was on caught fire and exploded off the coast of Brazil.

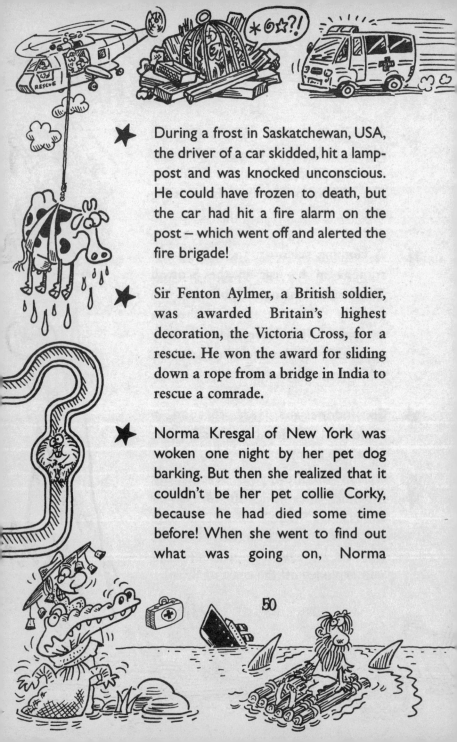

★ During a frost in Saskatchewan, USA, the driver of a car skidded, hit a lamp-post and was knocked unconscious. He could have frozen to death, but the car had hit a fire alarm on the post – which went off and alerted the fire brigade!

★ Sir Fenton Aylmer, a British soldier, was awarded Britain's highest decoration, the Victoria Cross, for a rescue. He won the award for sliding down a rope from a bridge in India to rescue a comrade.

★ Norma Kresgal of New York was woken one night by her pet dog barking. But then she realized that it couldn't be her pet collie Corky, because he had died some time before! When she went to find out what was going on, Norma

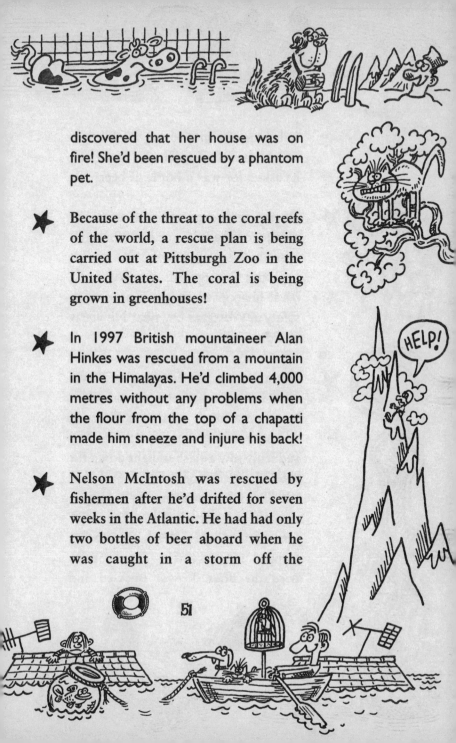

discovered that her house was on fire! She'd been rescued by a phantom pet.

⭐ Because of the threat to the coral reefs of the world, a rescue plan is being carried out at Pittsburgh Zoo in the United States. The coral is being grown in greenhouses!

⭐ In 1997 British mountaineer Alan Hinkes was rescued from a mountain in the Himalayas. He'd climbed 4,000 metres without any problems when the flour from the top of a chapatti made him sneeze and injure his back!

⭐ Nelson McIntosh was rescued by fishermen after he'd drifted for seven weeks in the Atlantic. He had had only two bottles of beer aboard when he was caught in a storm off the

HELP!

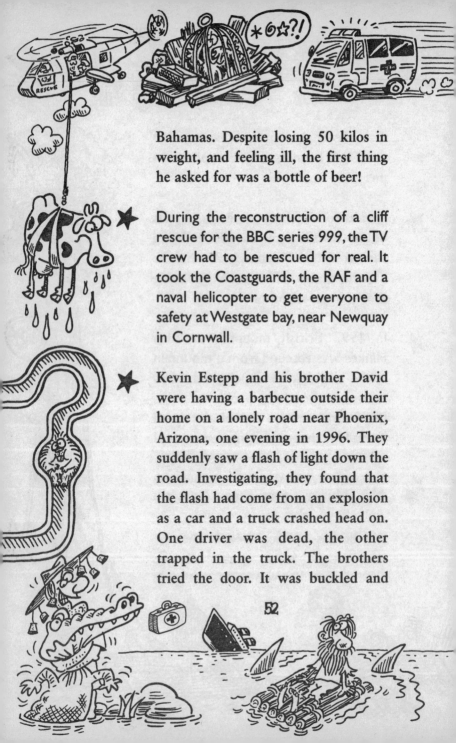

Bahamas. Despite losing 50 kilos in weight, and feeling ill, the first thing he asked for was a bottle of beer!

★ During the reconstruction of a cliff rescue for the BBC series 999, the TV crew had to be rescued for real. It took the Coastguards, the RAF and a naval helicopter to get everyone to safety at Westgate bay, near Newquay in Cornwall.

★ Kevin Estepp and his brother David were having a barbecue outside their home on a lonely road near Phoenix, Arizona, one evening in 1996. They suddenly saw a flash of light down the road. Investigating, they found that the flash had come from an explosion as a car and a truck crashed head on. One driver was dead, the other trapped in the truck. The brothers tried the door. It was buckled and

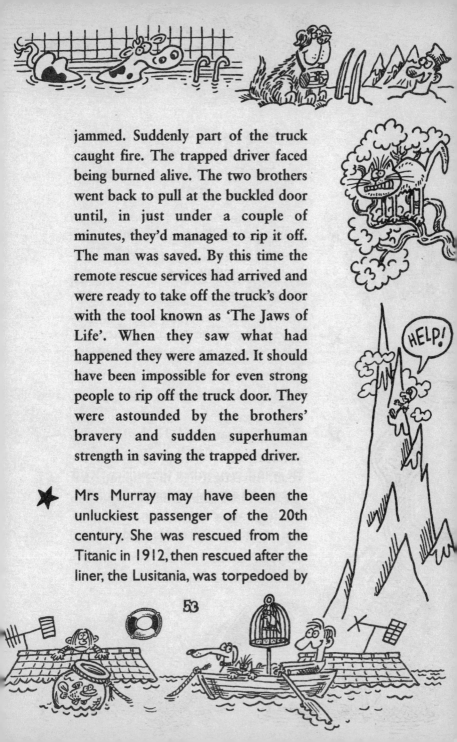

jammed. Suddenly part of the truck caught fire. The trapped driver faced being burned alive. The two brothers went back to pull at the buckled door until, in just under a couple of minutes, they'd managed to rip it off. The man was saved. By this time the remote rescue services had arrived and were ready to take off the truck's door with the tool known as 'The Jaws of Life'. When they saw what had happened they were amazed. It should have been impossible for even strong people to rip off the truck door. They were astounded by the brothers' bravery and sudden superhuman strength in saving the trapped driver.

★ Mrs Murray may have been the unluckiest passenger of the 20th century. She was rescued from the Titanic in 1912, then rescued after the liner, the Lusitania, was torpedoed by

HELP!

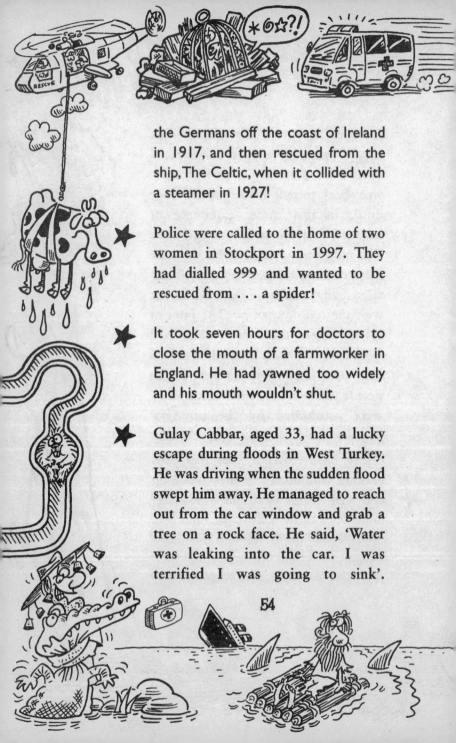

the Germans off the coast of Ireland in 1917, and then rescued from the ship, The Celtic, when it collided with a steamer in 1927!

⭐ Police were called to the home of two women in Stockport in 1997. They had dialled 999 and wanted to be rescued from . . . a spider!

⭐ It took seven hours for doctors to close the mouth of a farmworker in England. He had yawned too widely and his mouth wouldn't shut.

⭐ Gulay Cabbar, aged 33, had a lucky escape during floods in West Turkey. He was driving when the sudden flood swept him away. He managed to reach out from the car window and grab a tree on a rock face. He said, 'Water was leaking into the car. I was terrified I was going to sink'.

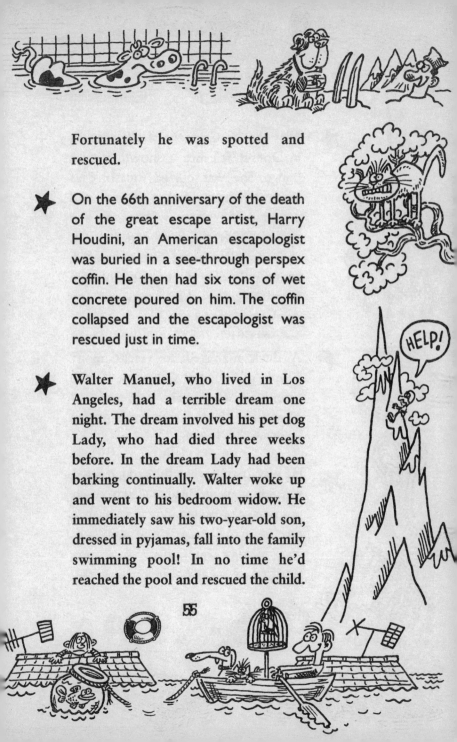

Fortunately he was spotted and rescued.

★ On the 66th anniversary of the death of the great escape artist, Harry Houdini, an American escapologist was buried in a see-through perspex coffin. He then had six tons of wet concrete poured on him. The coffin collapsed and the escapologist was rescued just in time.

★ Walter Manuel, who lived in Los Angeles, had a terrible dream one night. The dream involved his pet dog Lady, who had died three weeks before. In the dream Lady had been barking continually. Walter woke up and went to his bedroom widow. He immediately saw his two-year-old son, dressed in pyjamas, fall into the family swimming pool! In no time he'd reached the pool and rescued the child.

HELP!

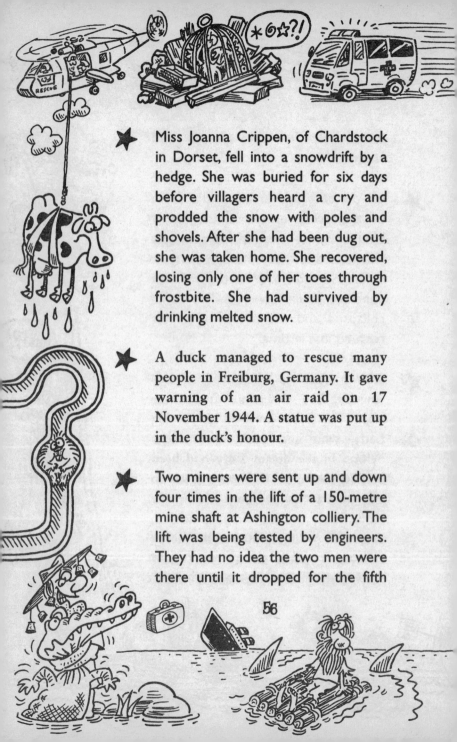

Miss Joanna Crippen, of Chardstock in Dorset, fell into a snowdrift by a hedge. She was buried for six days before villagers heard a cry and prodded the snow with poles and shovels. After she had been dug out, she was taken home. She recovered, losing only one of her toes through frostbite. She had survived by drinking melted snow.

A duck managed to rescue many people in Freiburg, Germany. It gave warning of an air raid on 17 November 1944. A statue was put up in the duck's honour.

Two miners were sent up and down four times in the lift of a 150-metre mine shaft at Ashington colliery. The lift was being tested by engineers. They had no idea the two men were there until it dropped for the fifth

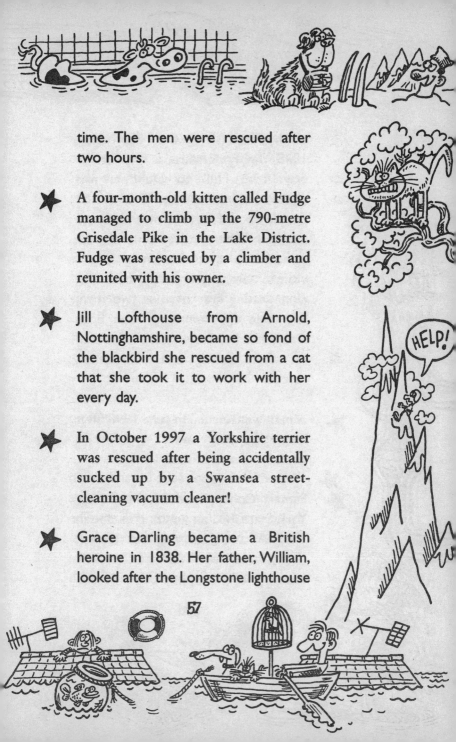

time. The men were rescued after two hours.

★ A four-month-old kitten called Fudge managed to climb up the 790-metre Grisedale Pike in the Lake District. Fudge was rescued by a climber and reunited with his owner.

★ Jill Lofthouse from Arnold, Nottinghamshire, became so fond of the blackbird she rescued from a cat that she took it to work with her every day.

★ In October 1997 a Yorkshire terrier was rescued after being accidentally sucked up by a Swansea street-cleaning vacuum cleaner!

★ Grace Darling became a British heroine in 1838. Her father, William, looked after the Longstone lighthouse

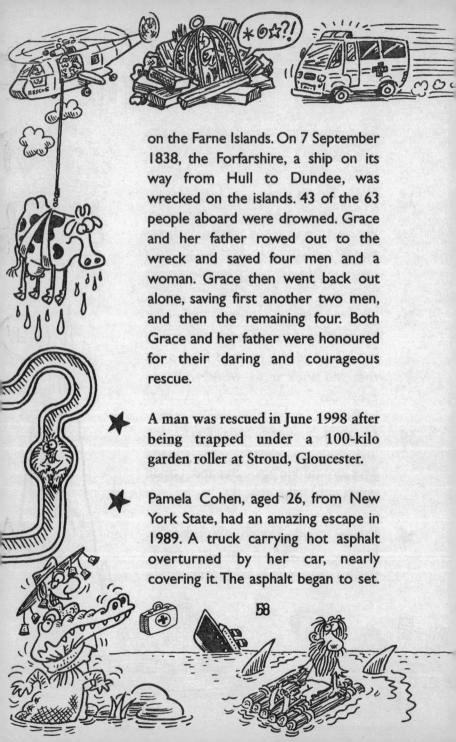

on the Farne Islands. On 7 September 1838, the Forfarshire, a ship on its way from Hull to Dundee, was wrecked on the islands. 43 of the 63 people aboard were drowned. Grace and her father rowed out to the wreck and saved four men and a woman. Grace then went back out alone, saving first another two men, and then the remaining four. Both Grace and her father were honoured for their daring and courageous rescue.

★ A man was rescued in June 1998 after being trapped under a 100-kilo garden roller at Stroud, Gloucester.

★ Pamela Cohen, aged 26, from New York State, had an amazing escape in 1989. A truck carrying hot asphalt overturned by her car, nearly covering it. The asphalt began to set.

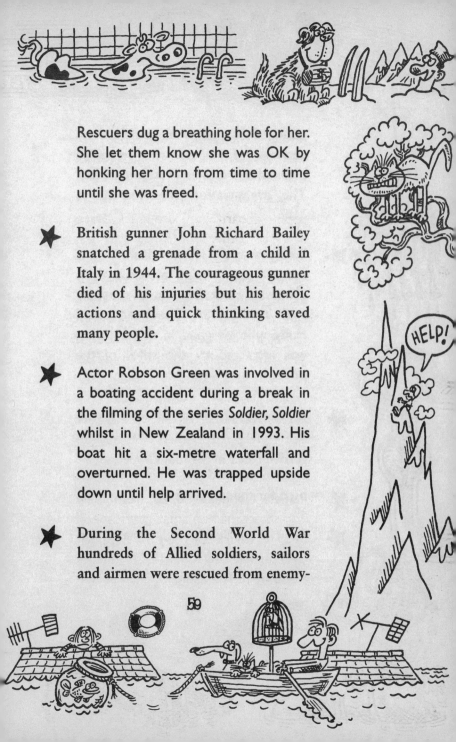

Rescuers dug a breathing hole for her. She let them know she was OK by honking her horn from time to time until she was freed.

★ British gunner John Richard Bailey snatched a grenade from a child in Italy in 1944. The courageous gunner died of his injuries but his heroic actions and quick thinking saved many people.

★ Actor Robson Green was involved in a boating accident during a break in the filming of the series *Soldier, Soldier* whilst in New Zealand in 1993. His boat hit a six-metre waterfall and overturned. He was trapped upside down until help arrived.

★ During the Second World War hundreds of Allied soldiers, sailors and airmen were rescued from enemy-

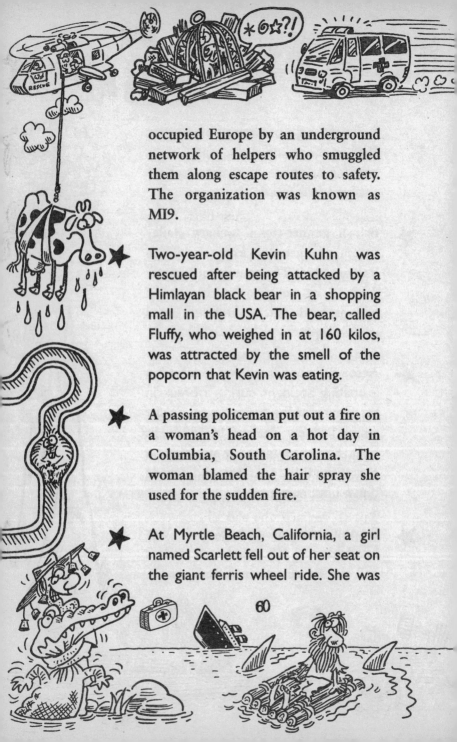

occupied Europe by an underground network of helpers who smuggled them along escape routes to safety. The organization was known as MI9.

Two-year-old Kevin Kuhn was rescued after being attacked by a Himlayan black bear in a shopping mall in the USA. The bear, called Fluffy, who weighed in at 160 kilos, was attracted by the smell of the popcorn that Kevin was eating.

A passing policeman put out a fire on a woman's head on a hot day in Columbia, South Carolina. The woman blamed the hair spray she used for the sudden fire.

At Myrtle Beach, California, a girl named Scarlett fell out of her seat on the giant ferris wheel ride. She was

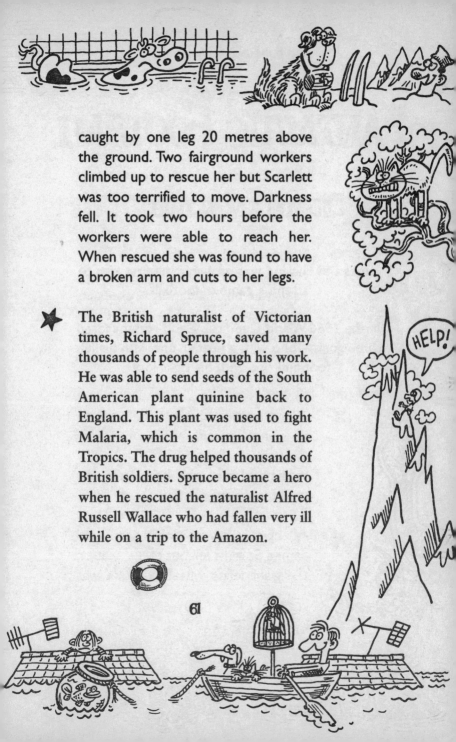

caught by one leg 20 metres above the ground. Two fairground workers climbed up to rescue her but Scarlett was too terrified to move. Darkness fell. It took two hours before the workers were able to reach her. When rescued she was found to have a broken arm and cuts to her legs.

★ The British naturalist of Victorian times, Richard Spruce, saved many thousands of people through his work. He was able to send seeds of the South American plant quinine back to England. This plant was used to fight Malaria, which is common in the Tropics. The drug helped thousands of British soldiers. Spruce became a hero when he rescued the naturalist Alfred Russell Wallace who had fallen very ill while on a trip to the Amazon.

Did you know that . . .

James I of England was probably the first king to
attend a game of football.

In the 1966 World Cup final, Geoff Hurst scored
three goals – one with a header, one with his left
foot and one with his right foot!

FACT ATTACK

BEASTLY BODIES

DID YOU KNOW THAT . . .

The human body loses enough heat in an hour to boil half a gallon of water.

If calcium is taken out of human bones, they become so rubbery that they can be tied in a knot like rope or string.

The city with the highest number of babies born in taxis is New York, USA.

A giraffe has the same number of bones in its neck as a human does.

Richard III of England, Louis XIV of France and the Emperor Napoleon of France were all born with teeth.

Fact Attack titles available from Macmillan

The prices shown below are correct at the time of going to press.
However, Macmillan Publishers reserve the right to show new retail prices
on covers which may differ from those previously advertised.

Awesome Aliens	0 330 35340 3	£1.99
Beastly Bodies	0 330 35341 1	£1.99
Cool Cars	0 330 35345 4	£1.99
Cracking Christmas	0 330 37504 0	£1.99
Crazy Creatures	0 330 35342 X	£1.99
Crucial Cricket	0 330 37498 2	£1.99
Dastardly Deeds	0 330 35344 6	£1.99
Deadly Deep	0 330 37500 8	£1.99
Devastating Dinosaurs	0 330 37495 8	£1.99
Dreadful Disasters	0 330 35347 0	£1.99
Fantastic Football	0 330 35343 8	£1.99
Gruesome Ghosts	0 330 35346 2	£1.99
Incredible Inventions	0 330 37494 X	£1.99
Mad Medicine	0 330 37082 0	£1.99
Magnificent Monarchs	0 330 37496 6	£1.99
Nutty Numbers	0 330 35434 5	£1.99
Remarkable Rescues	0 330 37502 4	£1.99
Rowdy Rugby	0 330 37501 6	£1.99
Spectacular Space	0 330 37497 4	£1.99
Super Spies	0 330 37499 0	£1.99
Vile Vampires	0 330 37503 2	£1.99

All Macmillan titles can be ordered at your local bookshop
or are available by post from:

**Book Service by Post
PO Box 29, Douglas, Isle of Man IM99 1BQ**

Credit cards accepted. For details:
Telephone: 01624 675137
Fax: 01624 670923
E-mail: bookshop@enterprise.net

Free postage and packing in the UK.
Overseas customers: add £1 per book (paperback)
and £3 per book (hardback).